I0437975

Good News for the Oppressed

The Spirit of the Sovereign LORD is upon me,
for the LORD has anointed me
to bring good news to the poor.
He has sent me to comfort the brokenhearted
and to proclaim that captives will be released
and prisoners will be freed.
He has sent me to tell those who mourn
that the time of the LORD's favor has come,
and with it, the day of God's anger against their enemies.
To all who mourn ...,
He will give a crown of beauty for ashes,
a joyous blessing instead of mourning,
festive praise instead of despair.
In their righteousness, they will be like great oaks
that the LORD has planted for his own glory.
Isaiah 61:1-3 NLT

**The purpose of this booklet is to share God's truth on Suicide
and to comfort the hearts of those who mourn.**

SUICIDE...THE UNPARDONABLE SIN?

VL Wilson

authorHOUSE®

AuthorHouse™
1663 Liberty Drive, Suite 200
Bloomington, IN 47403
www.authorhouse.com
Phone: 1-800-839-8640

First published by AuthorHouse 7/31/2008

ISBN: 978-1-4343-7581-0 (e)
ISBN: 978-1-4343-7580-3 (sc)

Library of Congress Control Number: 2008903215

Printed in the United States of America
Bloomington, Indiana

This book is printed on acid-free paper.

DEDICATION

This book is dedicated to those people who unselfishly interceded for me when I was in my deepest depression.

God knows your names. I felt your prayers.

Yulanda and A'Lexa, I owe you my sanity.

MY PRAYER

My prayer is that others would unselfishly pick up the mantle and pray for their loved ones, as these have done for me.

The prayer of a righteous man is powerful and effective. (NIV)

The earnest (heartfelt, continued) prayer of a righteous man

makes tremendous power available [dynamic in its working].
(AMP)

The prayer of a person living right with God

is something powerful to be reckoned with. (MSG)

The fervent effectual prayer of a righteous man availeth much!
(KJV)

SUICIDES BY STATE

(http://www.sprc.org/stateinformation/datasheets.asp)

Alabama – averages 3 suicides every 2 days
Alaska – averages 1 suicide every 3 days
Arizona – averages 11 suicides every 5 days
Arkansas - averages 1 suicide per day
California – averages 17 suicides every 2 day
Colorado – averages 13 suicides per week
Connecticut – averages 3 suicides every 4 days
Delaware – averages 1 suicide every 5 days
Florida – averages 6 suicides per day
Georgia – averages 5 suicides every 2 days
Hawaii – averages 2 suicides every 6 days
Idaho – averages 1 suicide every 2 days
Illinois – averages 3 suicides per day
Indiana – averages 2 suicides per day
Iowa – averages 7 suicides every 8 days
Kansas – averages 10 suicides every 11 days
Kentucky – averages 10 suicides every 7 days
Louisiana – averages 4 suicides every 3 days
Main – averages 3 suicides per week
Maryland – averages 5 suicides every 4 days
Massachusetts – averages 7 suicides every 6 days
Michigan – averages 20 suicides every 7 days
Minnesota – averages 4 suicides every 3 days
Mississippi – averages 9 suicides every 10 days
Missouri – averages 2 suicides per day
Montana – averages 2 suicides every 5 days
Nebraska – averages 1 suicide every 2 days
Nevada – averages 10 suicides every 9 days
New Hampshire – averages 1 suicide every 3 days
New Jersey – averages 3 suicides every 2 days
New Mexico – averages 1 suicide every day
New York – averages 13 suicides every 4 days
North Carolina – averages 8 suicides every 3 days
North Dakota – averages 1 suicide every 5 days
Ohio – averages 13 suicides every 4 days
Oklahoma – averages 4 suicides every 3 days
Oregon – averages 7 suicides every 5 days
Pennsylvania – averages 11 suicides every 3 days
Rhode Island – averages 1 suicide every 5 days
South Carolina – averages 5 suicides every 4 days
South Dakota – averages 1 suicide every 4 days
Tennessee – averages 2 suicides per day
Texas – averages 6 suicides per day

Utah – averages 6 suicides per week
Vermont – averages 1 suicide every 5 days
Virginia – averages 13 suicides every 6 days
Washington – averages 2 suicides per day
West Virginia – averages 5 suicides per week
Washington D.C. – averages 1 suicides every 11 days
Wisconsin – averages 5 suicides every 3 days
Wyoming – averages 1 suicide every 4 days

SUICIDE... the unpardonable sin?
Table of Contents

Section one:
Introduction:
Impetus for finding answers to those difficult questions
The Word established as our reference point.

Impetus for finding answers to those difficult questions

People used to talk all the time about how if you commit suicide, you cannot get into heaven. Usually, the reasoning went along the lines of "the person who committed suicide did not have a chance to repent of his sins." Something about this reasoning irked me. Perhaps it was that we don't confess all of our sins in order to get saved, so why would this be requisite to staying saved? Most of us on any given day have unconfessed sins in our lives; and if we were honest, sins of which we are truly not repentant. Not going to heaven because of unrepented sin, didn't seem right. However, and this is a big point -- is it true?

Can you lose your salvation? If so, what are the ways to lose your salvation? God explicitly states how to get saved. Does He make clear how to lose your salvation? Or is it 'once saved, always saved' as some believe? What about the unpardonable sin? Are there unpardonable sins (plural)?

These are all questions that require answers, and through the years I thought to research them. Then, tragedy brushed close to home. The issue of suicide became personal me and I determined to find the **truth**. My own son was found dead in his car, parked outside his backyard. The autopsy results were inconclusive. Was it accidental carbon monoxide poisoning, suicide, or foul play? The fact that he was not found in a garage or enclosed space or that one of his buddies had moved the body before calling the police, helped to "muddy the water." Still, the incident helped to ignite my need to find the truth. What does God say about suicide?

Despite the furor surrounding my sons death and my increased interest in what God had to say about suicide, it was only recently that God impressed upon me to write this book. He commanded me to "Take my yoke upon you and learn from me," which I did by daily by praying, studying His Word, and coming to know His mind on the matter. (Matt 11:29). I determined to discover the truth. God's word is truth. Therefore, putting personal feelings aside, I had to discover what God says on this issue of suicide.

The answers to these questions and a host of other related ones are found in this book. My prayer is that you will open your heart and receive God's word spoken through me. My prayer also is that you too, will find peace and that through the liberation of the word, help others who are weary and heavy laden with grief, find rest.

Where do we go for answers? Building a foundation in the Word.

God tells us in Hebrews 1:1-2, that in the <u>past</u>, He spoke to us through the prophets. In bygone days, when people wanted wisdom or direction, they went to the prophets through whom they received God's answers. We know that when the oppressed Israelites cried out to God because of the Midianites, He sent them a prophet to clarify things and give them direction. Judges 6:7-9. Time and again, the Israelites would need help or seek direction and a prophet would become available to answer the need. When Saul needed to know which way to go, they consulted a prophet or 'seer' as they were sometimes called. 1Samuel 9:8-10 And so it goes.

But what about *today?* Do we find our answers through the prophets? We can, but God gives us a better way. Better because it is a way open to anyone willing to find it. Today, God has chosen to speak to us through Jesus, His son.

> God, who at sundry times and in divers manners spake in time past unto the fathers by the prophets, hath in these last days spoken unto us by his Son, whom he hath appointed

heir of all things, by whom also he made the worlds; (Heb 1:1-2)

So, we look to Jesus. At face value, this doesn't seem to get us anywhere. *How* do we ask Jesus? God gave us a clue in the words above. God says that he is speaking to us through his son *who made the worlds*. John gives us more insight as he clearly shows that Jesus, the maker of the world, is also the Word. In the beginning, Jesus was with God and Jesus was God and through Jesus all things were made. Jesus is the Word.

> In the beginning was the Word, and the Word was <u>with</u> God, and the Word <u>was</u> God. He (the Word) was with God in the beginning. <u>Through him all things were made</u>; without him nothing was made that has been made. (John 1:1-3)

The Word, then becomes our final authority to discovering the truth the questions we seek. As we answer questions of suicide and the unpardonable sin, our foundational resource is the Word of God.

> John 17:17 Sanctify them through thy truth: thy **word is truth**.

> Psalm 33:4 For the **word of the Lord** is right;
> and all his works are done in truth.

Peter confirms our reliance on the word with:

"But the Word of the Lord (divine instruction, the Gospel) endures forever. And this Word is the good news which was preached to you." (1Peter 1:25, Amplified)

Since our foundation of truth is the Word of God, this is where we will go to get all of our answers.

Section two:
Suicide ... the unpardonable sin?
The Unpardonable sin
Blaspheming the Holy Spirit
The "Willful" sin
Suicide

The Unpardonable Sin

Is suicide the unpardonable sin? This is a very controversial subject, with people not only on both sides of the fence, but all over it. Nevertheless, it really doesn't matter what *we* believe. What matters is what God has to say. So the questions become, "What does God say about the unpardonable sin?" Let's turn to the bible, God's recorded word.

> Wherefore I say unto you, All manner of sin and blasphemy shall be forgiven unto men: but the blasphemy against the Holy Ghost shall not be forgiven unto men. (Matthew 12:31)

> I tell you the truth, all the sins and blasphemies of men will be forgiven them. But whoever blasphemes against the Holy Spirit will never be forgiven; he is guilty of an eternal sin." (Mark 4:28-29, NIV)

Let's review the context when Jesus spoke these words. He had just cast an unclean spirit out of someone and the then-churched leaders tried to say that Jesus was a devil himself and was casting out these demons by the power of the devil:

> 22 And the scribes which came down from Jerusalem said, He hath Beelzebub, and by the prince of the devils casteth he out devils.

> 23 And he called them unto him, and said unto them in parables, How can satan cast out satan?
> [Mark 3]

After a brief explanation on the impossibility of satan casting out himself, Jesus says the infamous words:

> 28 Verily I say unto you, All sins shall be forgiven unto the sons of men, and blasphemies wherewith soever they shall blaspheme:

> 29 But **he that shall blaspheme against the Holy Ghost hath never forgiveness, but is in danger of eternal damnation**.

> 30 Because they said, He hath an unclean spirit.

So it is clear that blaspheming the Holy Spirit is the unpardonable sin – the sin that has no forgiveness. The sin for which the person is in danger of eternal damnation.

Blaspheming the Holy Spirit

But what is blaspheming the Holy Spirit? Is it when we say that something that God ordains is devilish? Is it when we say that 'tongues' is from the devil when tongues is specifically specified from Paul, Peter and the other Apostles as a gift from the Holy Spirit? Is it when a TV evangelist heals someone and we say that the healing didn't come from God when it did? Or is it when we denigrate and laugh at how the Holy Spirit is moving through a person? Or is it when we talk about God's anointed, something that even the angels were afraid to do?

God forbid that it would be any of those things! If so, we would all be in danger of eternal damnation, for most of us have spoken foolishly and mistakenly about God at some point in our lives. No, as I continue, you'll see exactly what blaspheming is and who is and is not condemned for blaspheming.

First, let's look at who is not condemned for blaspheming. The unsaved are not; they are already condemned. Keep in mind that the ignorant unsaved are already going to hell. The sins they commit in their unsaved state are covered by the blood once they are saved. By definition, then it cannot be called *un- or not-pardonable*. The "unpardonable sin" as we've come to think of blaspheming the Holy Spirit is directed at the <u>saved</u> – those who have believed on the name of Jesus Christ. This was the first step in my understanding blaspheming the Holy Spirit – understanding for whom it did *not* apply. The unsaved are not in danger of eternal damnation, they are <u>guaranteed it</u>. You can't lose what you don't have. The scripture backs this up.

> 16 If any man **see his brother** sin a sin which is not unto death, he shall ask, and he shall give him life for them that sin not unto death. There is a sin unto death: I do not say that he shall pray for it.

> 17 All unrighteousness is sin: and there is a sin not unto death. [1 John 5]

.John spoke again of the unpardonable sin in 1John5. Notice the audience? It's a fellow Christian – a "brother" who is in danger of committing the unpardonable sin.

Paul illumines the sin more in Hebrews 10. At first this section utterly confused me. They brought me condemnation.

> 26 For if we sin wilfully after that we have received the knowledge of the truth, there remaineth no more sacrifice for sins,

> 27 But a certain fearful looking for of judgment and fiery indignation, which shall devour the adversaries.

Verse 26 tells me that if I sin on purpose after I know better, then I'm condemned. If willfully sinning (sinning because it was my will to do so … simply because I wanted to) is the criterion for condemnation, then I knew I was doomed. Most of us know what sin is and continue to do so – some out of habit, some out of simple disobedience. For instance, gluttony is a sin. I have gluttonized – ate that extra piece of cake – simply and solely because I wanted to – even when a small voice within me would say, "NO!". I have talked about people before when I knew not to. Why? because I wanted to. I have lied and cheated and stolen (I hasten to add *in the past*) because I wanted to.

So, verse 27 was dead on. I could understand why such a person who willfully sins fearfully looks over his shoulder for judgment and why he would harden his heart and be "indignant" about sin in a kind of "who are you to judge me" type of way. The person is already condemned, his heart feels it, so what's the use?

The next verses comment upon how severe a penalty we Christ-followers should get for deliberately sinning since our covenant is so much superior to Moses' ten commandments, since angels ratified his, but God himself ratified ours.

> 28 He that despised Moses' law died without mercy under two or three witnesses:

> 29 Of how much sorer punishment, suppose ye, shall he be thought worthy, who hath trodden under foot the Son of God, and hath counted the blood of the covenant, wherewith he was sanctified, an unholy thing, and hath done despite unto the Spirit of grace?

After these verses, my heart almost failed me. If willfully sinning after I was saved included my lying, cheating, hating (racism), being prejudiced (preferring one over another)… there was no hope. I'd participated in these as well as fornicating, drinking to drunkenness which led to debauchery, talking badly about God's anointed, and more.

> 30 For we know him that hath said, Vengeance belongeth unto me, I will recompense, saith the Lord. And again, The Lord shall judge his people.

This "judgment" or vengeance from God was what I feared all

along! And I truly could relate to the last part.

> 31 It is a fearful thing to fall into the hands of the living God.

It took me some time meditating on the Word for the truth to come out. The surface reading of these scriptures is misleading. I had to "study to show myself approved." So, I continued to pray and listen to the Holy Spirit. My not liking the scripture and being fearful of what it said, couldn't keep me from discovering the truth. My mission was to finally for all time, determine what God was saying. The Holy Spirit began to break the scripture down to me – word by word.

Looking closely at verses 29 helped me to <u>define</u> what sinning willfully was all about and my relief was profound! There are three ingredients revealed that lead to blaspheming the Holy Spirit. They are (a) troddening under foot the son of God; (b) counting the blood of the covenant as an unholy thing; and (c) despising the Spirit of grace. Let's break down these three ingredients. What do they really mean? We begin again in Hebrews 10, verse 29. [Note: Bracketed comments in the scriptures are mine]

> 29 Of how much sorer punishment, suppose ye, shall he be thought worthy, who

> 1. hath **trodden under foot the Son of God,**

> [*The Holy Spirit and I stopped here first. Trodden means to crush harshly, trample, walk over, etc. Under no circumstances would I desire to do that to Christ. Even when I'm sinning I'm not willfully treading underfoot the Son of God. I usually despise myself even as I'm in the midst of my sin I'm certainly not thinking on <u>any</u> level that Christ Jesus should be despised or was so worthless and beneath me that I could just crush, trample or walk over Him. Back to the scripture]*

2. and [he] hath **counted the blood of the covenant,** wherewith he was sanctified, **an unholy thing**

[*No way! I may sin, but I KNOW I'm sinning and am ashamed of it. I do <u>not</u> and never will count Jesus' blood an unholy thing. It's precious and I live because he died. I'm as grateful for that as anyone can be. I LOVE the Lord. I know He's Holy and good and His blood pure and precious.*]

3. and hath **done despite** unto the Spirit of grace?

[*Despite is contemptuous defiance, spite, and malice. The Spirit of Grace is God's gracious spirit. The Spirit that saw favor in us and gave and forgave us when we did not deserve to be. "Doing despite unto the Spirit of Grace" is synonymous with defiling and "blaspheming the Spirit." So then, doing despite unto the Spirit of grace is maliciously and spitefully spitting on the grace that the Spirit brings. The Message bible translation brings this out*]

> what do you think will happen if you turn on God's Son, spit on the sacrifice that made you whole, and insult this most gracious Spirit? This is <u>no light matter</u>. God has warned us that he'll hold us to account and make us pay. (verse 3)

That's when I realized something crucial. I would not purposefully do any of this! I would not purposefully do despite towards the Holy Spirit. I would not revile, execrate, denounce, or even think malice towards the Holy Spirit. If anything, I'm crying out to Him for help in the midst of my sins with all of my heart!]

What did we discover? Blaspheming the Holy Spirit, committing the unpardonable sin requires a <u>conscious</u> doing. To blaspheme is to "execrate" which is "to denounce, declare to be hateful" and the archaic meaning from Webster is to "invoke a curse on." No one can do these things accidentally. This is deliberate. This is willful hatred towards the Holy Spirit and all that He represents. This is willfully sinning. Ahhhhhh The light bulb goes off.

The *willful* sin is the unpardonable sin. As Paul confirms, it is *not* a light thing. It is a deliberate, evil, heartfelt thing. This verse broke for me the meaning of "sin willfully." And I knew beyond a shadow of a doubt that I had not and never intend to commit such an act. Blaspheming the Holy Spirit as I now saw was anathema to me. Not only that (but bringing in what we learned earlier) it is a willful conscious choice <u>of believers</u> –those people who have received God, tasted and seen His goodness, and reject him outright – knowingly and consciously.

Let's look back to John. He understood this.

> 16 If any man **see his brother** sin a sin which is not unto death, he shall ask, and he shall give him life for them that sin not unto death. There is a sin unto death: I do not say that he shall pray for it.
>
> 17 All unrighteousness is sin: and there is a sin **not** unto death. [1 John 5]

The "Willful" sin

There's a difference between sinning that is unrighteousness – lying, cheating, fornicating, greed, envy, idolatry, etc and the willful, unpardonable sin that is 'unto death,' such as execrating all over the Holy Spirit. Someone who sins but even as he/she does so hates his sin as much as God does is not committing the unpardonable sin. The spirit is willing but the flesh is weak. That's bad – the sin can even be horrific -- but it's not the unpardonable sin.

Those saved people who are tormented over what they are doing are indeed sinning, but not unto death. God wants to give those people peace and has provided them with a way out. These are the "poor in Spirit." They need to see God. They need a revelation of who He is in them. But this type of person – even when the sin is recurring like a bad habit – is *not* committing the unpardonable sin. They are children of God. Their hearts do not hate and despise the Lord. They do not want to spit on and cast underfoot Christ. They do not entertain the thought that Jesus blood is evil and unholy. NO, these people – of which I am one – need God and want God. They are not blaspheming Him.

Let me give you a perfect illustration of someone committing the unpardonable sin. I was going to make one up, but I remembered hearing this true story about a Pastor's wife sin and it could not be more appropriate:

This Pastor was married to a beautiful woman who had always wanted to be an actress, but gave up her dream for him. Her husband's call to minister hindered her life's dream. At first she was OK with the decision. She loved her husband, the Pastor and loved God. But, as time went on, she grumbled and complained at her "sacrifice." An "imp" would sit on her shoulder, whispering in her ear how ungrateful her husband was and how much of a sacrifice it had truly been for her. As she listened to the imp, she became more and more discontented until she was consumed with her lost opportunity. By then, the imp had gone through her ear and had its arms wrapped around her brain. The woman stopped praying and only grudgingly went to church. *[Realize that at this point, though sinning, she had not yet committed the unpardonable sin!]* Soon her days were obsessed with becoming an actress and her hatred of all things Christian. One day she yelled out to God that Jesus had ruined her life. She told

Him to "Get out!" At that point the demonic imp dropped from her head into her spirit.

Now this entire time, her husband had been praying for her and eliciting the help of others including a prophet friend of his. But at the time when his wife told Jesus to "Get Out" God gave the prophet a vision. He went to the Pastor and told him to stop praying for his wife. She was lost for good. The prophet saw the "imp" and what had happened in the vision. He also saw her plummet to hell, screaming all the way. Blaspheming the Spirit led to eternal damnation.

Did you see at what point she blasphemed the Holy Spirit? As I was remembering this scenario, the Holy Spirit spoke to me these words: **"She had invited Jesus into her heart with a confession and invited Him out of her heart the same way -- The one with tears and humility, the other with hatred and malice."** I could see it then. This woman had been saved, had understood Jesus and salvation, but swallowed a lie and exchanged the glory of God for that lie. She voluntarily and with great malice, execrated the Holy Spirit. She met all three steps necessary for blaspheming the Holy Spirit as outlined in Hebrews 10. She willfully

1. hath **trodden under foot the Son of God;**

2. and hath **counted the blood of the covenant,** wherewith he was sanctified, **an unholy thing;** and

3. and hath **done despite** unto the Spirit of grace

We finally understood the unpardonable sin and it makes the last part of Hebrews 10 even clearer to me:

30For we know him that hath said, Vengeance belongeth unto me, I will recompense, saith the Lord. And again, The Lord **shall judge his people.**

31It is a fearful thing to fall into the hands of the living God.

Suicide

Let's bring this home to suicide.

The majority of people who commit suicide are not consciously and deliberately rejecting Christ. They are rejecting their lives and trying to escape the horribleness of circumstances – whether physically, mentally, or emotionally. They have been deceived. They <u>have sinned</u> in taking their own life. They <u>have sinned</u> in not trusting and believing in God enough – to trust that He could and would make a way for them when there seemed to be no way. But they did *not* commit the unpardonable sin, AND they did not reject Christ.

The three ingredients necessary for blaspheming the Holy Spirit are not met in the suicide; eternal damnation is not accrued.

1. hath **trodden under foot the Son of God**;

2. and hath **counted the blood of the covenant**, wherewith he was sanctified, **an unholy thing**; and

3. and hath **done despite** unto the Spirit of grace

Any of us who have ever had thoughts of suicide, no matter how fleeting, know that we were not rejecting Christ; we did not think his sacrifice unholy. If anything, we were deceived for a time into thinking that we were not worthy to accept God's gift of grace.

The suicidal person can be forgiven. That person did not commit the unpardonable sin, and. as Paul let us know, all other sin is forgivable.

> Wherefore I say unto you, All manner of sin and blasphemy shall be forgiven unto men: but the blasphemy against the Holy Ghost shall not be forgiven unto men. (Matthew 12:31)

Therefore, while still a sin, suicide is one of those other "manner of sins." The kind that *can* be forgiven.

Section three:
The Question: How do you "Lose" your salvation? Can you lose your salvation through Suicide?
Losing your Salvation

"Losing" your Salvation

The confusion over whether someone can lose their salvation is one of semantics. Let's look back at the illustration of the Pastor's wife who let bitterness engulf her to the extent that she lost sight of God's goodness and rejected God's Spirit to the point that she even rejected Christ's salvation work (Section 2). Did she lose her salvation or did she throw it away? She discarded it. It was a willful act. You don't "lose" your salvation, but you can indeed give it back. The difference is the deliberateness of the act of the unpardonable sin.

You don't blaspheme the Holy Spirit by accident. You don't accidentally go too far. In the natural, among men, you can accidentally "go too far," but not with God. His gracious Spirit allows His love to cover a multitude of our sins. Blaspheming the Holy Spirit, as we saw through the scriptures (Section 2) is a deliberate action. It is not based on ignorance (as what happens when we call acts instigated by the Holy Spirit demonic or of the flesh such as speaking in tongues or a miraculous healing), but a meanness and wickedness of spirit. To blaspheme or discard your salvation you consciously despise the Holy Spirit – spit on him and on the cross; and you mean the curse or action to the core of your being.

While suicide is a deliberate act of sin, it is not an act of spitting on the cross and all it represents. The vast majority of suicidal people are looking for a way out – looking for peace. They are seeking a way – a better place – in order to get out of the torment of their current situation. They most definitely are not purposefully rejecting Christ. The ones who commit suicide are deceived. If we could hear the cry of their heart, it would not be "I hate you, Jesus," but "Where are you, Jesus?"

On the other hand, while you may not have heard the blasphemous people cry to God to get out of their lives like the Pastor' wife, they did it and _meant_ it. The actions that you see of them (the once Christian) consciously choosing to sin with no remorse or care about God at all is the fruit borne from their evil spirit within. They have castigated God which makes the first part of Hebrews 10 all the more meaningful:

> 26 For if we sin wilfully **after** that we have received the knowledge of the truth, there remaineth no more sacrifice for sins,

> 27 But a certain fearful looking for of judgment and fiery indignation, which shall devour the adversaries.

These blaspheming people are willfully sinning ones who once proclaimed the truth, but now defecate all over it. What hope then is there for them? They are not going to Christ for forgiveness. They are not confessing their sins to Him to be cleansed as 1 John 5 promises. No, they despise Christ and spit on his blood. There then "remains no more sacrifice" for them. [Suicide victims do not fall into this category.] But all that the blasphemous folks can look for is judgment. It's over for them. There is a sin that leads to death – willful rejection of Christ; and there are sins that don't.

The bottom line is once saved is _not_ always saved. While the other foundational truth is you don't lose it, you (with conscious abandon) refuse it.

Again, regarding suicide, I repeat with emphasis the words written beforehand:

> People who commit suicide are not consciously and deliberately rejecting Christ. They are rejecting their lives and trying to escape the horribleness of

circumstances – whether physically, mentally, or emotionally. They have been deceived. They have sinned in taking their own life. They have sinned in not trusting and believing in God enough – to trust that He could and would make a way for them when there seemed to be no way. But they did not commit the unpardonable sin AND they did not reject Christ.

Section four:
Is suicide forgivable before God?
Does God forgive the sin of suicide?

Does God forgive the sin of suicide?

> "Therefore I say to you, **any** sin and blasphemy
> shall be forgiven people, but blasphemy against
> the Spirit shall not be forgiven.
>
> "Whoever speaks a word against the Son of Man,
> it shall be forgiven him; but whoever speaks
> against the Holy Spirit, it shall not be forgiven
> him, either in this age or in the age to come.
> (Mark 3: 28-29)

Clearly, suicide does not fall into the unforgivable, unpardonable
sin category. Verse 31 is explicit. "*Any* sin and blasphemy shall be
forgiven people." It doesn't say 'some' sins, but 'any' sin. The only
exception is blaspheming the Holy Spirit, which we fully discussed
earlier.

If you were in doubt, remember the sin that is not forgiven is the
sin of speaking against through rejecting the Holy Spirit.

> but whoever speaks against the Holy Spirit, it shall
> not be forgiven him, either in this age or in the age
> to come. (vs 32)

Suicide does not fall under this jurisdiction of defined by the
unforgiven sin; suicide does not fall into the realm of "speaking
against the Holy Spirit.".

But, Suicide **is** a sin. Let's be very clear. While, suicide is indeed a
sin, it is not the unpardonable, unforgivable one. As we saw that
John stated:

16 If any man see his brother **sin a sin which is not unto death**, he shall ask, and he shall give him life for them that sin not unto death. There is a sin unto death: I do not say that he shall pray for it.

17 **All** unrighteousness is sin: and **there is a sin not unto death**. [1 John 5]

Suicide is a sin, but not one that leads to death, eg. eternal damnation.
As Paul says: "… that He (Jesus) is the means to forgiveness of sins is backed up by the witness of all the prophets." Acts 10:39, MSG

Section five:
Is suicide a mortal sin?
What about the 'unconfessed sin' nature of suicide?
The Mortal sin
Unconfessed sin

The Mortal sin

Catholics and many Protestants believe that Suicide is a mortal sin. The early church did not share this view Martyrs were almost revered before this time and many Christians erroneously thought suicide was the way to gain favor and show the depth of Christ love. St. Augustine brought into vogue the unpardonable nature of suicide sin around the end of 5th or early 6th century. It was not a biblical foundational truth. In 1983, the Vatican relented on suicide and extended the caveat that if a person was not in their 'right' or 'sound' mind at the time of the act, they could get a Christian burial.

The idea of suicide being a mortal sin was a man-made tradition. Human traditions are fine, but they cannot be acknowledged or revered MORE THAN the Word of God. Jesus frowns on this: Mark 7:8 NIV "You have let go of the commands of God and are holding on to the traditions of men." We must not fall into this same trap of letting go of the Word of God in order to embrace our tradition or religious belief.

The bible says that there are sins leading to death and sins not (1John 5:16-17). Which ones they are not specifically stated. We only know for certain what is the unpardonable sin. That was clearly dealt with in Matthew 12: 30-32. [See Unpardonable Sin section.]. And even in 1John, when we closely examine John's words, we see that suicide is not a sin that leads to death.

> 16 If any man see his brother **sin a sin which is not unto death**, he shall ask, and he shall give him life

for them that sin not unto death. There is a sin unto death: I do not say that he shall pray for it.

If you read closely, you see that a fellow Christian has to see his brother committing the sin, and then pray for him. No one sees the brother committing suicide, and once the deed is done; there is no further need to pray for him. The man/woman is dead. Whatever the sins John is talking about, suicide can be ruled out.

Let's be clear. Suicide is a sin. That is unequivocal. "Though shalt not kill" guarantees this. Then there are the very real arguments that you belong now to Christ, your life is not your own -- which means you do not have the right to take it. There is also the argument that now that you have turned the Lordship of your life to Jesus, He is Lord, not you. That means that He has the right to end your life or continue your life because of your submission to His will, and not yours.

Yes, suicide is a sin. It is a committed usually by those overwhelmed with pain and persons who cannot see their way out of a situation. These people have stopped trusting God for that instance and it cost them dearly. This too is a sin – not trusting God. Nevertheless, it is NOT a mortal, nor an unpardonable one.

> "Therefore I say to you, **any** sin and blasphemy shall be forgiven people, but blasphemy against the Spirit shall not be forgiven. (Mark 3:28)

Unconfessed sin

But what about the Unconfessed nature of the sin of suicide?

> If we claim to be without sin, we deceive ourselves and the truth is not in us. If we confess our sins, he is faithful and just and will forgive us our sins and purify us from all unrighteousness. (1 John 8-9)

Many people believe that suicide is unforgiven, _because_ it is not confessed. What does the Word say?

While it is certainly true that confessed sin is forgiven, the converse is not true. There are many sins in a person's life that they have not confessed (or repented of). There are slights that people have done to you; there are grudges people hold; there are accidental and deliberate sins that we have committed and swept under the rug. No one has confessed and asked for forgiveness for every sin that they have committed. This is *impossible.*

What is possible is that every sin is wiped clean by the blood of Jesus, and this is an act of salvation. Jesus' blood shed for us is the reason we are forgiven. Jesus died for us. In Matthew 26:28, Jesus tells us that his blood is poured out for the forgiveness of our sins. Acts 10:43 lets us know that through Jesus, the forgiveness of sins is proclaimed. Notice that throughout the bible it is 'sins' plural. Jesus forgives all sins. On the cross, he said, "It is finished." All sins, one act. A Christian's sins are forgiven, past, present, and future at the cross.

In Romans we get even greater clarity. Paul lets us know that by identifying with Christ, the Messiah – the second Adam, we are freed from all of our sins *at* the cross. The gift that God gives us through Jesus is that our many offences are declared righteous through his death and resurrection.

> 15 But, not as the offence so also [is] the free gift;
> for if by the offence of the one the many did die,
> much more did the grace of God, and the free gift
> in grace of the one man Jesus Christ, abound to the
> many;
>
> 16 and not as through one who did sin [is] the
> free gift, for the judgment indeed [is] of one to
> condemnation, but the gift [is] of many offences to
> a declaration of `Righteous,'

But here's the real crux of the matter. Through our confession of faith, we are cleansed and freed from our sin. The confession is *not* of our sins, it's our confession of faith in the redemptive work of Christ Jesus. We're confessing with our faith aloud because, "if you confess with your mouth that Jesus is Lord and believe in your heart that God raised him from the dead, you will be saved." (Romans 10:9) This then is how salvation is won and how it's kept – through faith.

> But what saith it? The word is nigh thee, even in thy mouth, and in thy heart: that is, the word of faith, which we preach; (Romans 10:8)

> 9 That if thou shalt confess with thy mouth the Lord Jesus, and shalt believe in thine heart that God hath raised him from the dead, thou shalt be saved.

Colossians 1:14. In Him, we have redemption, the forgiveness of sins.

Adding to salvation the rule that we must have confessed every sin before we die is a "works" mentality. We cannot earn our way to heaven . Salvation is not based on us, but on Him.

> "For it is by grace you have been saved, through faith—and this not from yourselves, it is the gift of God— 9not by works, so that no one can boast." (Ephesians 2:8-9)

As Paul so eloquently states for the Christian Jesus is the one who died for us, he doesn't condemn us. Who can bring charges against the Christian and *make them stick*? No one. Through the Blood, we're justified. Our guilt / sin is pardoned, not because we confess each and every single act we've done before we die, but because we believe that Jesus paid the price for us in totality. *His* act, our freedom.

> If God is for us, who can be against us? He who did not spare his own Son, but gave him up for us all—how will he not also, along with him, graciously give us all things? Who will bring any charge

23

against those whom God has chosen? <u>It is God who justifies</u>. Who is he that condemns? Christ Jesus, who died—more than that, who was raised to life—is at the right hand of God and is also interceding for us. Who shall separate us from the love of Christ? Shall trouble or hardship or persecution or famine or nakedness or danger or sword? ... No, in all these things we are more than conquerors through him who loved us. For I am convinced that neither death nor life, neither angels nor demons, neither the present nor the future, nor any powers, neither height nor depth, nor anything else in all creation, will be able to separate us from the love of God that is in Christ Jesus our Lord. (Romans 8: 31-39, NIV)

Section six:
Understanding the Suicidal Mentality
One Day at a Time

One Day at a Time

The thing that suicidal / depressed people do not realize and what clouds their thinking is the overwhelming futility of life. The vastness of their problems overtake them and any help seems insignificant – a drop in the bucket of need. Instead of taking one day, one hour, one moment at a time, they look down the road and think: "Twas ever thus, twill ever be." It's hopeless. My circumstances will remain this way until eternity. They do not see that you *have* to live each day one day at a time. Any more is too much for them. The suicidal person can't handle it and are crushed under the "hopeless" load.

> "Sufficient unto the day is the evil thereof."
> (Matthew 6:34).

There is enough going on in <u>one</u> day for any person to deal with. The "sane" person realizes that their failures are to be shouldered one day at a time – that as horrible as *today* may seem, tomorrow can be better. Each day is a new day to start over. The suicidal person loses sight of the ebb and flow of life. The tragedies of the day are the tragedies of a lifetime. That thinking is debilitating. Our minds can't take the extra stress – especially when we're down. Most people realize that they don't have to combat loneliness for a life time -- just one day at a time. The adulterer or fornicator don't 'have to be pure and not commit sexual sins for a month or even a week – just simply today -- Just this hour -- Just this second. That is why God identified Himself to Moses as the "I Am." He is present tense -- in the moment. He is "a very present help in times of trouble" (Ps 46:1). That's God. He helps and keeps us moment by moment.

It's liberating for me to be able to say, "Thank you God for keeping me today. I'm not promising tomorrow, but today is cool." God meets me where I am, just as He meets you and the rest of mankind. Suicidal people don't realize it.

The suicidal person cannot see the forest (of free grace, mercy, and forgiveness) for the trees (sin and shame). They can only see their problem(s). They are overwhelming. They want peace and deliverance and do not know how to get it. They do not realize that in the middle of a drinking binge, they can say "Help." And God will hear them.

A suicidal person is the most self-absorbed person there is because the world has literally stopped to revolve solely around them and their issues. They can't see past themselves. God is not enthroned in *now* greatness. The present-help aspect of God is lost on the suicidal person. There is no help outside of themselves. Everything is about them. This is sinful and dangerous because they are blind to the light – the very thing / person who could help save them.

This self-absorption truly hits on the sin-aspect of suicide. A person who is self-absorbed has put SELF on the throne of his, admittedly screwed world. It is wicked to dethrone God and put yourself in His place, which is what we do every time we put *our* will and *our* choice above God's. When we refuse to trust Him, we decide He is a liar and untrustworthy. We know best. It doesn't work. There is no peace for the wicked. The suicidal person is without peace, constantly tormented, and without hope because the One who is Hope has been discarded or dethroned. God is no longer Lord. This is sin. This is troubling. So is the resulting loss of faith in God. Suicide is the by-product.

Section seven:
Death and Life: Life and Death
Consequences for actions
Life and Life more abundantly

Consequences for Actions

> For the wages of sin is death,
> but the gift of God is eternal life in Christ Jesus our Lord
> Romans 6:23

Though the world seems to belittle consequences to actions,
it doesn't negate the fact that God imposes them. Thankfully,
the consequence for the person who commits suicide is not the
ultimate spiritual death. Still, he loses out on life. He loses out on
fulfilling the plans that God had for him. A good spiritual analogy
that God himself gives us through Paul (Peter) is that of the man
who built upon God's foundation wood, hay and stubble. In other
words, sin, selfishness, greed, etc. The bible says that person will
be saved, but as though he had gone through fire and was burned.
Painful, yes, but infinitely preferable to the damnation of hellfire.

> But if any person's work is burned up [under the
> test], he will suffer the loss [of it all, losing his
> reward], though he himself will be **saved**, but only
> as [one who has passed] through **fire**. (1 Cor 3:15)

Yes, there are consequences to our choices and our disobedience to
our Father God, but thankfully, being disowned is not one of them.

We all have those times when we doubt or put our will and
beliefs over and above what God has to say. Usually, however, the
consequences our loss/lack of faith is not so dire. You do not always
know the consequences for your actions and as humans, we always
believe we will get another chance. The sobering fact is that the

future is not promised you. The I AM God only promises you the present. If the man who had been robbed had known the hour that the robber would have come, he would have kept his house secure (Matthew 24:43). Hindsight.

> I have set before you life and death, blessings and
> curses.
> Now choose life, so that you and your children may
> live
> Deut 30:19, NIV

God puts the choice before us on how to live. It's His way as described in the Word or the world's way. Along with actions come reactions, blessings or cursings. God gives us a push in the right direction when He tells us to choose life so that we can live. Still, in a myriad of ways, we choose death and cursings all the time.

The suicidal person did not begin suicidal. The person who commits suicide chose sin, which led to death (consequence). Thank God for God's gift of everlasting life, so that even though the mortal body is gone, the suicidal person's soul/spirit lives on. To be absent from the Body is to be present with the Lord (2 Corinthians 5:8).

Life and Life more Abundantly

Know that there is a plan and purpose for your loved ones lives.

> For I know the plans I have for you," declares the
> LORD, "plans to prosper you and not to harm
> you, plans to give you hope and a future. (Jeremiah
> 29:11)

Remind the suicidal person of this. Jesus came to give your loved ones more abundant life. It's one thing to 'live' as in 'survive.' It's another to LIVE. Quality of life is important to God. He doesn't want to see His children barely existing from day to day. In this sense, I am not talking financial, but being emotionally bankrupt – without hope, simply enduring.

My sister and I have an expression "Holding our breath." We realize that this doesn't' work. You cannot merely hold your breath from one catastrophe to another. That's not quality of life. You're just holding on in your own strength. You're really relying on you, and that breaks down after a while -- which is not only sad and sinful, but also un-sustainable. You can only "pull yourself up from your bootstraps" for so long. Eventually you get to the end of your strength, which is why we can't be our own God and have life and life more abundantly. That's a gift from God through Jesus.

God wants you to enter into His rest where He holds on *for* you. That's part of our deliverance parcel from Christ, the messiah. Trust God and live.

I once had a friend who was really into self-help – which is good and has its place – but is bad when taken to extreme. You can't self-help your way into self-actualization to God or to attain Godlike status (a child of God through your own righteousness, will, or self-improvement). Suicidal persons have discovered this harshly. They've come halfway to enlightenment. They realize that if all there is themselves – they are doomed. They have come to the end of themselves and starkly see it isn't enough.

What they fail to do is look outside of themselves and trust God. If you seek Him with your whole heart -- not half-stepping or only allowing in the God that conforms to your theology -- you will find Him. The suicidal person realizes they alone are not enough, but fails to put God back on the throne. So he is without help, without hope, and hopeless.

It didn't have to be and doesn't have to be. Remind your suicidal ones of this.

If we claim to be without sin, we deceive ourselves and the truth is not in us. If we confess our sins, he is faithful and just and will forgive us our sins and purify us from all unrighteousness (1John 1:8-9).

The Message bible includes the phrase "He won't let us down."

On the other hand, if we admit our sins—make a clean breast of them—he won't let us down; he'll be true to himself. He'll forgive our sins and purge us of all wrongdoing.

Section eight:
Help for the Suicidal
What you can do?
Be Patient: God answers prayer

What you can do?

So, what can you do to help the suicidal person? The depressed person? The downtrodden person? The answer most people give is ... "Pray!" But that seemed like such a mamby pamby answer to me. Prayer. But then I received the revelation -- *Not* prayer, but **intercession**. Prayer is to Intercession like a pebble is to a boulder.

So what is intercession, and how do you do it? Intercession is warfare prayer. It is a deep, prayer that allows you, the stronger person, to stand in the place of the weaker, suicidal one and (a) withstand the pain for them, giving them a breather, a chance to "come back into their right mind; (b) fight the demons or demonic attack for a time for them so that they can regroup and come back fighting; and/or (c) take the blinders from before their eyes so that they can stand back and really see the truth of their situation. They might be in desperate straights, but there is hope. Sometimes depression has such a grip on someone that their minds are clouded and confused. People can really be "not in their right mind." These people need a stronger person to stand in the gap for them to receive and provide – to combat the spiritual forces that are at work battling them and attempting to destroy them. This is intercession -- sustaining the weak through the prayer of the strong.

God says, "give us this day our daily bread." The bread is whatever the person needs. The bread could be something physical, mental, spiritual or financial. The intercessor pulls down the bread that the suicidal person desperately needs, but cannot attain on his own. Through intercession, you take back ground from the enemy or opposing forces that have been gained from your loved one. It's giving the loved one the help that he/she needs, but is incapable (for whatever reason) of getting for themselves. This is intercession.

Intercession is not for the weak. Jesus made and continually makes intercession for us:

> Who is he that condemneth? It is Christ that died, yea rather, that is risen again, who is even at the right hand of God, who also maketh **intercession** for us. Romans 8:34

So does the Holy Spirit:

> Likewise the Spirit also helpeth our infirmities: for we know not what we should pray for as we ought: but the Spirit itself maketh **intercession** for us with groanings which cannot be uttered.

> And he that searcheth the hearts knoweth what is the mind of the Spirit, because he maketh **intercession** for the saints according to the will of God.

Intercession is a mighty war instrument, used primarily to keep those weaker from succumbing to death due to a stronger foe. Jesus and the Holy Spirit make intercession for us so that we can remain strong down here on earth. The spirit is willing, but the flesh is weak. Intercession is powerful: "The fervent effectual prayer of a righteous man availeth much."(James 5:16b). Intercession is effective.

Have you ever asked yourself why some people die and some don't? During the Tsunami of a few years back. Were those people more wicked than everyone else? Were the New Orleans people that bad? **Was your loved one who committed suicide or the loved one that is contemplating it a worse sinner than all others?** No, Jesus specifically answers this question in Luke chapter 13, starting in verse one. He tells us what to do, and gives an illustration with him interceding and delivering someone. Watch: Luke 13:1-3

> About that time some people came up and told him
> (Jesus) about the Galileans Pilate had killed while
> they were at worship, mixing their blood with the
> blood of the sacrifices on the altar.

Here's the question.

> Jesus responded, "Do you think those murdered
> Galileans were worse sinners than all other
> Galileans?

Here's the answer.

> Not at all. Unless you turn to God, you, too, will die.

And in case the point was not made, Jesus repeats:

> And those eighteen in Jerusalem the other day, the
> ones crushed and killed when the Tower of Siloam
> collapsed and fell on them, do you think they were
> worse citizens than all other Jerusalemites? Not at
> all. Unless you turn to God, you, too, will die."

Those people and our loved ones who die tragically are *not* worse
sinners. We all need to turn to God or we will be in the same
boat. No, that's _life_, living in a cursed or "fallen" world. Bad things
happen.

BUT Here's the *hope*. There is something that we can do about it.
Jesus goes on to tell how we can intercede on behalf of the person
who is doomed or in a calamity – such as deep depression or any
other mind or body debilitating reason. Listen.

> Then he (Jesus) told them a story: "A man had an
> apple tree planted in his front yard. He came to it
> expecting to find apples, but there weren't any. He
> said to his gardener, 'What's going on here? For
> three years now I've come to this tree expecting
> apples and not one apple have I found. Chop it

down! Why waste good ground with it any longer?'
(Luke 13:6-7)

The man represented the destroyer or opposition. This man is ready to bring calamity on the tree, which represents the unfruitful person. Suicidal people feel that their life is fruitless and it's pointless to go on. It doesn't matter if this isn't reality. It's reality to *them*! So, our fruitless loved one -- whether through rebellion, whether by their own deeds or because of things that have happened to them – stands there limply, unfruitful, ready to die. The net result is that he or she hasn't been producing for a while. Now here you can come. You're the gardener.

> "The gardener said, 'Let's give it another year. I'll dig around it and fertilize, and maybe it will produce next year; if it doesn't, then chop it down.'" (vs 8-9)

The gardener intercedes on the behalf of the loved one. He under-girds the tree and brings it the nutrients (bread) that it needs. The intercessor is humble enough to spend quality time helping the tree. He commits himself for a year, if necessary. We can do no less for our loved one. We have to be serious to pray and intercede on his behalf. At first, you may not see any growth. But you continue to pray for the individual in faith. It may be inconvenient at times. You may simply be tired or not in the mood to lay down your life for this person and labor on his behalf. But if someone doesn't, then the tree (your loved one) gets cut down. In other worlds, with no one's hand there to stay the execution, death comes.

In intercession, we pray deliverance down. Then we can go to the person ourselves or God can move someone else to and the person can be physically delivered. Why do you think Jesus went out early in the morning or late at night to pray so much? He was praying our needs down, so that we – who did not have the ability to meet our own needs – could be delivered, healed, have peace, etc. We're doing the same thing for our family members, friends, or loved ones, especially those deep in depression or suicide. They cannot help themselves. Drugs, alcohol, chemical imbalance, hearing voices, horrific past experiences – whatever it is that was the catalyst for a clouded, confused mind, doesn't matter. As I said before, it doesn't matter if it was their fault or not. Through intercession, that person can be delivered and set free.

It's not a coincidence that right after teaching the parable of the intercessing gardener, Jesus goes into the healing of the woman who had been sick for many years:

> And, behold, there was a woman which had a spirit
> of infirmity eighteen years, and was bowed together,
> and <u>could in no wise lift up herself</u>. (Luke 13:11)

She couldn't help herself. She had a spirit of infirmity for quite a long time. But Jesus was her intercessor. Though some religious people were against her and she didn't find help in the church, she found help through Jesus, the intercessor.

> And ought not this woman, being a daughter
> of Abraham, whom Satan hath bound, lo, these
> eighteen years, be loosed from this bond on the
> sabbath day? (vs 16)

He loosed or freed her from her predicament. It didn't matter how long she'd been imprisoned. He delivered her. We can do the same for those we know who are infirm in their spirits, their minds, or their bodies.

I have personally been at the point where I would have welcomed suicide as a relief from the pain of living. Because of a series of adverse circumstances that just pummeled me in that they fell back to back to back of each other, I felt like living was too hard. From November to March, my son died, I was raped, my dad died, and I lost one of my best friends. It was too much. I simply wanted to go "home" to heaven. In my depressed and confused state, I turned to alcohol for some relief. I couldn't face getting through a 24 hour day. It hurt to breathe. I tried to sleep as much as I could as a means of escape. I'd work long and hard and drink my way through the evening and night. Yes, I was saved. Yes, I was filled with the Spirit. And even at my lowest point, I would cling to God with all that was within me. The salient point was there wasn't much *in* me. I was depleted. I felt like Lot. I needed help.

I needed an intercessor. Thankfully, people <u>were</u> praying for me; I could *feel* their prayers in my more lucid moments. One day, I simply "woke up," and I realized more fully that the prayers of those unselfish enough to labor for me had pulled me through. By gradual degrees, I came back completely to myself. Do not underestimate the power of prayer – your intercessory prayer. It makes a difference. James 5:16 in the Amplified says, "The earnest (heartfelt, continued) prayer of a righteous man makes tremendous power available [dynamic in its working]." Believe it.

Be Patient: God answers prayer

You will have need of patience. Just remember, God does answer prayer. Don't think that God isn't working out your situation. Don't think when you don't see an immediate change in the situation that nothing is happening. God is dealing with the issues *from the root.* **THIS** is where your faith comes in. Your faith is simply in trusting that He *is* doing something about the situation – even when it doesn't look like it.

God gave us an excellent example of this in Mark. One day, Jesus breathed the prayer for the fig tree to be cursed. While the answer came immediately, the outside world could not see it. It wasn't until the next day that the disciples noticed that the fig tree was "withered from the root." Let's take a look [*Bracketed words are mine!]*

The Cursed Fig Tree (Mark 11:12-21, nlt)

The next morning as they [*Jesus and the disciples*] were leaving Bethany, Jesus was hungry. He noticed a fig tree in full leaf a little way off, so he went over to see if he could find any figs. But there were only leaves because it was too early in the season for fruit. Then Jesus said to the tree, "May no one ever eat your fruit again!" And the disciples heard him say it. [*This is where Jesus spoke the word to change his circumstances Morning of Day one.*]

When they [*Jesus and the disciples*] arrived back in Jerusalem, Jesus entered the Temple and began to drive out the people buying and selling animals for sacrifices. He knocked over the tables of the money changers and the chairs of those selling doves, and he stopped everyone from using the Temple as a marketplace. He said to them, "The Scriptures declare, 'My Temple will be called a house of prayer for all nations,' but you have turned it into a den of thieves." When the leading priests and teachers of religious law heard what Jesus had done, they began planning how to kill him. But they were afraid of him because the people were so amazed at his teaching.

That evening Jesus and the disciples left the city. [*Notice that Jesus and the disciples leave to return home. A full day of activity had commenced. Nothing was noteworthy about the fig tree. No change was obvious. Evening of Day one*]

The next morning as they passed by the fig tree he had cursed, the disciples noticed it had withered from the roots up. [*ahhhh, now something is evident to the disciples. Day two.*] Peter remembered what Jesus had said to the tree on the previous day and exclaimed, "Look, Rabbi! The fig tree you cursed has withered and died!"

Then Jesus concludes the lesson of the fig tree with this admonition Then Jesus said to the disciples, "Have faith in God. I tell you the truth, you can say to this mountain, 'May you be lifted up and thrown into the sea,' and it will happen. But you must really believe it will happen and have no doubt in your heart. I tell you, you can pray for anything, and if you believe that you've received it, it will be yours. But when you are praying, first forgive anyone you are holding a grudge against, so that your Father in heaven will forgive your sins, too."

The other encouraging word from Jesus is that He told us to "Have faith in God." We can't change the problems in our loved ones lives (or even our own), but God can (and will). You don't have to have strength and faith on your own to change any circumstances.

God's timing and God's ways are not like ours. God's ways are higher than our ways and His thoughts higher than our thoughts (Isaiah 55:9). We have to take that to heart. God doesn't THINK the same way we do or act (an extension of thinking) the same way we do. He is thorough. He does not half step. He corrects, cleans, fees, delivers, expunges – all and all from the inside out. Just like the tree that Jesus commanded to be withered by the roots, our loved one's lives will be cleansed from the roots. That's especially heart-warming to those who have ever picked weeds. Weeds pulled from the roots are gone for good.

My God is an awesome God.

Section nine:
Bible Suicides
Definition of Suicide
Suicide accounts in the Bible

Definition of Suicide

Broadly speaking suicide is when someone takes his own life.
Usually we think of it as a direct, intentional action or link from
one event to another. A person was severely depressed, so she shot
herself (like Ahithophel, who hanged himself in despair because
his request to kill David was denied (2 Samuel17). Or because a
person was scared to face the consequences of his actions, he gored
himself -- like King Zimri of Tirzah who torched himself when
he saw he was surrounded and would have to pay for his crimes of
treason (1 Kings 16). Assisted suicide is considered suicide where
the person was too weak (emotionally or physically) and directly
asked for help, assistance in completing the deed. Two Kings Saul
(1 Samuel 31) and Abimilech (Judges 9), both asked their armor
bearers to kill them.

Suicide:
the/an act of killing oneself deliberately
(Kernerman English Multilingual Dictionary)

Assisted Suicide:
accomplished with the aid of another person, especially a
physician. (American Heritage Dictionary)

When someone knows that cigarette smoking causes cancer and
continues to smoke, is she committing suicide? If the doctor
tells you that if you continue to eat X and you continue, are you
committing suicide? If the wages of sin is death, and you keep
sinning are you committing suicide? How directly must the action
be linked to the final deed for the event to be designated suicide?

Most often, the root cause of those who commit suicide is depression as evidenced by Saul's life; his kingdom reign ended in ruin (1 Samuel 31) or extreme sorrow or guilt like Judas who betrayed Jesus and could not live with himself afterwards (Matthew 27). Pride and cowardice are other reasons, as shown through Abimelech King of Israel's actions when he begged his armor bearer to kill him because he did not want to be remembered as the King who died at a woman's hand. Nevertheless, there have been noble instances of suicides, such as blind Sampson (Judges) who committed suicide in part to defeat his kinsmen's foe as he deliberately knocked down the pillars to which he was chained and killed thousands of the philistines along with himself. Admittedly, revenge played a huge part in this, but the nobility aspect is real.

Suicide accounts in the Bible

Seven direct suicides are outlines seven accounts of suicide in the bible. These are those who directly took their life

Abimelech
Judges 9:50-55

Pride: Abimelech did not want to die by the hand of a woman.

Next Abimelech went to Thebez and besieged it and captured it. Inside the city, however, was a strong tower, to which all the men and women—all the people of the city—fled. They locked themselves in and climbed up on the tower roof. Abimelech went to the tower and stormed it. But as he approached the entrance to the tower to set it on fire, a woman dropped an upper millstone on his head and cracked his skull.

Hurriedly he called to his armor-bearer, "Draw your sword and kill me, so that they can't say, 'A woman killed him.' "So his servant ran him through, and he died. When the Israelites saw that Abimelech was dead, they went home (NIV).

Sampson

Judges 16:25-31

Revenge: Sampson wanted revenge for the loss of his eyesight and ridicule at the hands of his enemy the Philistines.

And it came to pass, when their hearts were merry, that they said, Call for Samson, that he may make us sport. And they called for Samson out of the prison house; and he made them sport: and they set him between the pillars.

And Samson said unto the lad that held him by the hand, Suffer me that I may feel the pillars whereupon the house standeth, that I may lean upon them.

Now the house was full of men and women; and all the lords of the Philistines were there; and there were upon the roof about three thousand men and women, that beheld while Samson made sport.

And Samson called unto the LORD, and said, O Lord God, remember me, I pray thee, and strengthen me, I pray thee, only this once, O God, that I may be at once avenged of the Philistines for my two eyes.

And Samson took hold of the two middle pillars upon which the house stood, and on which it was borne up, of the one with his right hand, and of the other with his left.

And Samson said, Let me die with the Philistines. And he bowed himself with all his might; and the house fell upon the lords, and upon all the people that were therein. So the dead which he slew at his death were more than they which he slew in his life.

Then his brethren and all the house of his father came down, and took him, and brought him up, and buried him between Zorah and Eshtaol in the buryingplace of Manoah his father. And he judged Israel twenty years. (KJV)

Saul
1 Samuel 31: 1-4

<u>Fear and Failure</u>: Saul was in deep depression as he had just lost all of his family in the battle and was about to lose his life. Seeing nothing but capture, Saul feared being tortured and ridiculed by his enemies the Philistines. This combination of fear and failure led to his suicide

> *Now the Philistines attacked Israel, and the men of Israel fled before them. Many were slaughtered on the slopes of Mount Gilboa. The Philistines closed in on Saul and his sons, and they killed three of his sons— Jonathan, Abinadab, and Malkishua. The fighting grew very fierce around Saul, and the Philistine archers caught up with him and wounded him severely. Saul groaned to his armor bearer, "Take your sword and kill me before these pagan Philistines come to run me through and taunt and torture me." But his armor bearer was afraid and would not do it. So Saul took his own sword and fell on it. (NLT)*

Saul's armor-bearer
1 Samuel 31:5

<u>Impulse</u>: Saul's armor-bearer, who had just watched his King commit suicide, wanted to join him. According to Christian Answers Network, Saul's armor-bearer's death was a direct result of impulse (http://www.christiananswers.net/q-dml/dml-y038.html). This is not rare; they report that 40% of teenage suicide is due to impulse.

> *When his armor bearer realized that Saul was dead, he fell on his own sword and died beside the king. (NLT)*

Ahithophel
2 Samuel 17:4-7,
11, 14, 23

<u>Pride</u>: Ahithophel was insulted that his admittedly superior advice to Absolon did not carry weight.

This plan seemed good to Absalom and to all the elders of Israel.

But Absalom said, "Summon also Hushai the Arkite, so we can hear what he has to say." When Hushai came to him, Absalom said, "Ahithophel has given this advice. Should we do what he says? If not, give us your opinion."

Hushai replied to Absalom, "The advice Ahithophel has given is not good this time... So, I advise ...

Absalom and all the men of Israel said, "The advice of Hushai the Arkite is better than that of Ahithophel." For the LORD had determined to frustrate the good advice of Ahithophel in order to bring disaster on Absalom.

When Ahithophel saw that his advice had not been followed, he saddled his donkey and set out for his house in his hometown. He put his house in order and then hanged himself. So he died and was buried in his father's tomb. (NIV)

Zimri
1 Kings
16:15-19

Fear: Zimri was afraid to experience the consequences of his treasonous actions.

Zimri began to rule over Israel in the twenty-seventh year of King Asa's reign in Judah, but his reign in Tirzah lasted only seven days. The army of Israel was then attacking the Philistine town of Gibbethon. When they heard that Zimri had committed treason and had assassinated the king, that very day they chose Omri, commander of the army, as the new king of Israel.

So Omri led the entire army of Israel up from Gibbethon to attack Tirzah, Israel's capital. When Zimri saw that the city had been taken, he went into the citadel of the palace and burned it down over himself and died in the flames. For he, too, had done what was evil in the LORD's sight. He followed the example of Jeroboam in all the sins he had committed and led Israel to commit. (NLT)

Judas
Matthew 27:3-5

Guilt and Remorse: Judas betrayed Jesus and could not see a way to undo the damage that he had done.

When Judas, who had betrayed him, saw that Jesus was condemned, he was seized with remorse and returned the thirty silver coins to the chief priests and the elders. "I have sinned," he said, "for I have betrayed innocent blood."

"What is that to us?" they replied. "That's your responsibility."

So Judas threw the money into the temple and left. Then he went away and hanged himself. (NIV)

The above have been straightforward cases of suicide. Nevertheless, there are other biblical accounts of those who have asked God to kill them. Thankfully, in each account, God did not comply; however, depending upon the depth of sincerity of their request, these accounts fall under the heading of 'attempted suicides.' The key is "Did they mean it?" Like Job, many of us have thought about suicide, but the thought was fleeing. There was no intent to follow-through.

When Job was in such pain, he cried out: I would rather be strangled—rather die than suffer like this. I hate my life and don't want to go on living. Oh, leave me alone for my few remaining days." (Job 7:15-16, NLT). However, none of his actions impressed me as true suicidal. His were the ramblings of the severely distraught. The Philippians' jailor on the other hand only stayed his hand because of Paul's intervention. He would have followed through on his actions to pierce him by his sword, fearing the consequence of dereliction of duty. He thought that the prisoners has escaped when God opened the prison doors.

Moses **Numbers** **11:12-15**	<u>Overburdened and discouraged</u>: Moses was depressed in his overwhelming job with ungrateful and troublesome subordinates:

Have I conceived all this people? Have I brought them forth, that You should say to me, Carry them in your bosom, as a nursing father carries the sucking child, to the land which You swore to their fathers [to give them]?

Where should I get meat to give to all these people? For they weep before me and say, Give us meat, that we may eat.

I am not able to carry all these people alone, because the burden is too heavy for me.

And if this is the way You deal with me, kill me, I pray You, at once, and be granting me a favor and let me not see my wretchedness [in the failure of all my efforts]. (AMP)

Elijah
1 Kings
19:1-4

<u>Depression and Fear</u>: Elijah was scared for his life and depressed.

Now Ahab told Jezebel everything Elijah had done and how he had killed all the prophets with the sword. So Jezebel sent a messenger to Elijah to say, "May the gods deal with me, be it ever so severely, if by this time tomorrow I do not make your life like that of one of them."

Elijah was afraid and ran for his life. When he came to Beersheba in Judah, he left his servant there, while he himself went a day's journey into the desert. He came to a broom tree, sat down under it and prayed that he might die. "I have had enough, LORD," he said. "Take my life; I am no better than my ancestors." (NIV)

Jonah
Jonah
3:114:1-11

<u>Rebellion and unforgiveness</u>: Jonah did not want to obey God or see his mercy.

And should not I spare Nineveh, that great city, wherein are more than sixscore thousand persons that cannot discern between their right hand and their left hand; and also much cattle?

But it displeased Jonah exceedingly, and he was very angry.

And he prayed unto the LORD, and said, I pray thee, O LORD, was not this my saying, when I was yet in my country? Therefore I fled before unto Tarshish: for I knew that thou art a gracious God, and merciful, slow to anger, and of great kindness, and repentest thee of the evil.

Therefore now, O LORD, take, I beseech thee, my life from me; for it is better for me to die than to live.

**Philippians'
Jailor**
Acts 16:
25-30

Fear: The Jailor in Philippians was fearful of his life.

Around midnight Paul and Silas were praying and singing hymns to God, and the other prisoners were listening. Suddenly, there was a massive earthquake, and the prison was shaken to its foundations. All the doors immediately flew open, and the chains of every prisoner fell off! The jailer woke up to see the prison doors wide open. He assumed the prisoners had escaped, so he drew his sword to kill himself. But Paul shouted to him, "Stop! Don't kill yourself! We are all here!"

The jailer called for lights and ran to the dungeon and fell down trembling before Paul and Silas. Then he brought them out and asked, "Sirs, what must I do to be saved?" (NLT)

Section ten:
Bible Suicides
Suicide Facts At A Glance – Center for Disease Control
Contacts: Online support groups and discussion boards

Suicide Facts at a Glance

These are Suicide facts published by the Center for Disease in the summer of 2007. More information can be found at http://www.cdc.gov/ncipc/dvp/suicide/suicidedatasheet.pdf

Fatal Suicidal Behavior	Gender Disparities
In 2004: • Suicide was the eleventh leading cause of death for all ages (CDC 2005). • Suicides accounted for 1.4% of all deaths in the U.S. (CDC 2005). • More than 32,000 suicides occurred in the U.S. This is the equivalent of 89 suicides per day; one suicide every 16 minutes or 11.05 suicides per 100,000 population (CDC 2005). • The National Violent Death Reporting System examined toxicology tests of those who committed suicide in 13 states: 33.3% tested positive for alcohol; 16.4% for opiates; 9.4% for cocaine; 7.7% for marijuana; and 3.9% for amphetamines (Karch et al. 2006).	• Males take their own lives at nearly four times the rate of females and represent 78.8% of all U.S. suicides (CDC 2005). • During their lifetime, women attempt suicide about two to three times as often as men (Krug et al. 2002). • Suicide is the eighth leading cause of death for males and the sixteenth leading cause for females (CDC 2005). • Among males, adults ages 75 years and older have the highest rate of suicide (rate 37.4 per 100,000 population) (CDC 2005). • Among females, those in their 40s and 50s have the highest rate of suicide (rate 8.0 per 100,000 population) (CDC 2005). • Firearms are the most commonly used method of suicide among males (56.8%) (CDC 2005). • Poisoning is the most common method

Nonfatal Suicidal Thoughts and Behavior	Racial and Ethnic Disparities
• Among young adults ages 15 to 24 years old, there is 1 suicide for every 100-200 attempts (Goldsmith et al. 2002). • Among adults ages 65 years and older, there is 1 suicide for every 4 suicide attempts (Goldsmith et al. 2002). • In 2005, 16.9% of U.S. high school students reported that they had seriously considered attempting suicide during the 12 months preceding the survey. More than 8% of students reported that they had actually attempted suicide one or more times during the same period (Eaton et al. 2006).	• Among American Indians/Alaska Natives ages 15- to 34-years, suicide is the second leading cause of death (CDC 2005). • Suicide rates among American Indian/Alaskan Native adolescents and young adults ages 15 to 34 (21.4 per 100,000) are 1.9 times higher than the national average for that age group (11.5 per 100,000). (CDC 2005). • Hispanic female high school students in grades 9-12 reported a higher percentage of suicide attempts (14.9%) than their White, non-Hispanic (9.3%) or Black, non-Hispanic (9.8%) counterparts. (Eaton et al. 2006).
Nonfatal, Self-Inflicted Injuries*	**Age Group Differences**
• In 2005, 372,722 people were treated in emergency departments for self-inflicted injuries (McCaig 2006). • In 2005, 154,598 people were hospitalized due to self-inflicted injury (CDC 2005). • There is one suicide for every 25 attempted suicides (Goldsmith et al. 2002). **The term "self-inflicted injuries" refers to suicidal and non-suicidal behaviors such as self-mutilation*	• Suicide is the second leading cause of death among 25-34 year olds and the third leading cause of death among 15- and 24-year olds (CDC 2005). • Among 15- to 24-year olds, suicide accounts for 12.9% of all deaths annually (CDC 2005). • The rate of suicide for adults aged 65 years and older was 14.3 per 100,000 (CDC 2005).

Suicide-Related Behaviors among U.S. High School Students	References
In 2005: • 16.9% of students, grade 9-12, seriously considered suicide in the previous 12 months (21.8% of females and 12.0% of males) (Eaton et al. 2006). • 8.4% of students reported making at least one suicide attempt in the previous 12 months (10.8% of females and 6.0% of males) (Eaton et al. 2006). • 2.3% of students reported making at least one suicide attempt in the previous 12 months that required medical attention (2.9% of females and 1.8% of males) (Eaton et al. 2006). .	1. Centers for Disease Control and Prevention (CDC). Web-based Injury Statistics Query and Reporting System (WISQARS) [Online]. (2005). National Center for Injury Prevention and Control, CDC (producer). Available from URL: www.cdc.gov/ncipc/wisqars/default.htm. 2. Karch D, Crosby A, Simon T. Toxicology testing and results for suicide victims—13 States, 2004. MMWR 2006; 55:1245-8. 3. Eaton DK, Kann L, Kinchen SA, Ross JG, Hawkins J, Harris WA, et al. Youth risk behavior surveillance—United States, 2005. MMWR 2006; 55(No. SS-5):1-108. 4. Goldsmith SK, Pellmar TC, Kleinman AM, Bunney WE, editors. Reducing suicide: a national imperative. Washington (DC): National Academy Press; 2002. 5. Krug EG, Dahlberg LL, Mercy JA, Zwi A, Lozano R, editors. World report on violence and health. Geneva: World Health Organization; 2002. 6. McCaig LF, Nawar EN. National hospital ambulatory medical care survey: 2004 emergency department summary. Advance data from vital and health statistics. Hyattsville (MD): National Center for Health Statistics; 2006. Report no. 372.

For more information, please contact:
Centers for Disease Control and Prevention
National Center for Injury Prevention and Control
1-800-CDC-INFO • www.cdc.gov/injury • cdcinfo@cdc.gov

Contacts: Online support groups and discussion boards

Christian Survivors
http://www.christiansurvivors.com/index2.html

Christians in pain
http://christianpain.faithweb.com/

Christians in Recovery
http://christians-in-recovery.org/links/Links/Christian/Suicide/

Contemplating suicide?
www.behindthebadge.net/suicide/index.html

Jesus Loves You Too
http://www.jesuslovesu2.com/suicide/suicide3.htm

Lamplight
http://www.yourlifecounts.org/index.aspx

Problems of Life
www.soon.org.uk/problems/suicide.htm

Samaritans
www.samaritans.org

Suicide. ... is not the way out!
www.bungechord.com/suicide

Suicide Crisis Center
http://suicide.com/suicidecrisiscenter/

Suicide
www.suicidal.com

Suicide: Gateway to Peace?

http://members.aol.com/wnichint/Suicide.html

Survivors Road to Healing
http://www.road2healing.com/

Walking wounded.net
http://www.walking-wounded.net/